Our Old Nursery Rhymes

A COLLECTION OF FAVORITE NURSERY RHYMES

Illustrated by

HENRIETTE WILLEBEEK LE MAIR

PHILOMEL BOOKS

New York

A NOTE ABOUT THE ORIGINAL EDITION

Our Old Nursery Rhymes was first published in 1911, when Henriette Willebeek le Mair was twenty-two. It was le Mair's fourth book and along with its companion, *Little Songs Of Long Ago* (1912), established le Mair's international reputation. The original book contained musical arrangements and slight differences in artwork and design, but its feeling and content was very much like the book we publish today.

Copyright © 1989 by Soefi Stichting Inayat Fundatie Sirdar.
Published in the United States in 1989 by Philomel Books,
a division of The Putnam & Grosset Group,
200 Madison Avenue, New York, NY 10016.
Published simultaneously in Canada.
Originally published by Gallery Children's Books,
an imprint of East-West Publications (UK) Ltd., London.
All rights reserved.
Printed in Hong Kong by South China Printing Co.
Library of Congress Cataloging-in-Publication Data
LeMair, Henriette Willebeek. Our old nursery rhymes
Henriette Willebeek Le Mari (i.e. Mair). p.   cm.
Summary: Presents a collection of thirty traditional nursery rhymes.
1. Nursery rhymes. 2. Children's poetry. [1. Nursery rhymes.]
1. Title. PZ8.3.L53950u 1989 398′.8−dc19 88-25530 CIP
ISBN 0-399-21722-3
First impression

Contents

Little Bo-Peep 5

Dance a Baby Diddy 7

Mary, Mary, Quite Contrary 9

What Are Little Boys Made Of? 11

Little Jack Horner 13

O Dear, What Can the Matter Be? 15

I Love Little Pussy 17

Lucy Locket 19

Mary Had a Little Lamb 21

Goosey, Goosey, Gander 23

Baa, Baa, Black Sheep 25

Jack and Jill 27

Here We Go Round the Mulberry Bush 29

The North Wind Doth Blow 31

Little Boy Blue 33

Humpty Dumpty 35

Oh Where, Oh Where Has My Little
  Dog Gone? 37

Dance to Your Daddy 39

Yankee Doodle 41

Three Little Kittens 43

Three Blind Mice 45

Young Lambs to Sell 47

Pussy Cat, Pussy Cat 49

Ding, Dong, Bell 51

Georgie Porgie 53

Ride a Cock Horse 55

Little Miss Muffett 57

There Was a Little Man 59

Polly Put the Kettle On 61

Hush-a-Bye Baby 63

Index of First Lines 64

Little Bo-Peep

Little Bo-Peep has lost her sheep,
    And can't tell where to find them,
Leave them alone
And they'll come home,
Bringing their tails behind them.

Little Bo-Peep fell fast asleep,
And dreamt she heard them bleating;
    But when she awoke,
    She found it a joke,
For they were still a-fleeting.

Then up she took her little crook,
Determined for to find them;
    She found them indeed,
    But it made her heart bleed,
For they'd left their tails behind them.

It happened one day, as Bo-Peep did stray
Into a meadow hard by,
    There she espied
    Their tails side by side,
All hung on a tree to dry.

She heaved a sigh, and wiped her eye,
And over the hillocks went rambling.
    And tried what she could,
    As a shepherdess should,
To tack again each to its lambkin.

Dance a Baby Diddy

Dance a baby, diddy,
   What can mammy do wid' e,
But sit in her lap,
   And give 'un some pap,
And dance a baby diddy?

Mary, Mary, Quite Contrary

Mary, Mary, quite contrary,
How does your garden grow?
With silver bells and cockle shells,
And pretty maids all in a row.

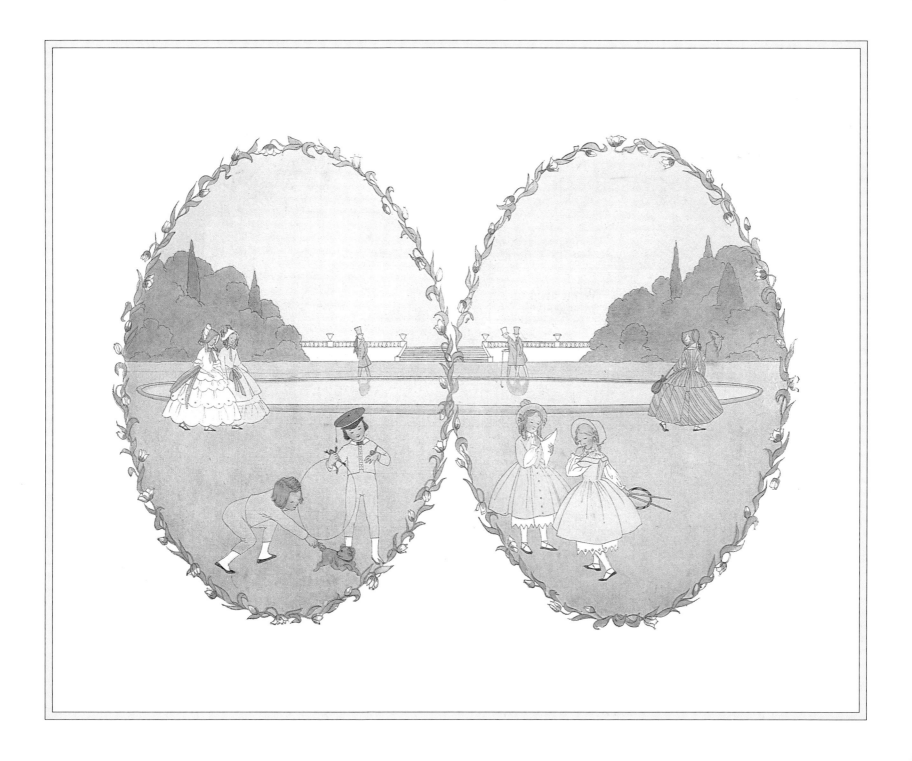

What Are Little Boys Made Of?

What are little boys made of?
   What are little boys made of?
Frogs and snails and puppy-dogs' tails,
   That's what little boys are made of.

What are little girls made of?
   What are little girls made of?
Sugar and spice and all that's nice,
   That's what little girls are made of.

What are our young men made of?
   What are our young men made of?
Sighs and leers and crocodile tears,
   That's what our young men are made of.

What are young women made of?
   What are young women made of?
Ribbons and laces and sweet pretty faces,
   That's what young women are made of.

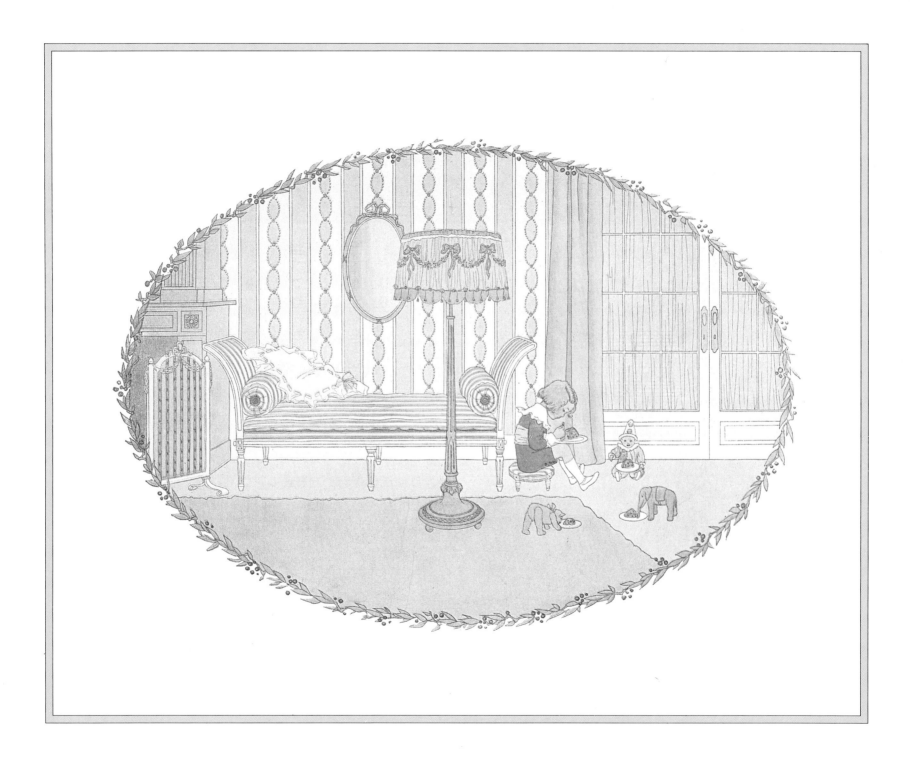

Little Jack Horner

Little Jack Horner
  Sat in the corner,
Eating a Christmas pie;
  He put in his thumb,
    And pulled out a plum,
And said, What a good boy am I!

O Dear, What Can the Matter Be?

O dear, what can the matter be?
　　Dear, dear, what can the matter be?
O dear, what can the matter be?
　　Johnny's so long at the fair.

He promised he'd bring me a basket of posies,
　　A garland of lilies, a garland of roses,
He promised to bring me a bunch of blue ribbons
　　To tie up my bonny brown hair.

I Love Little Pussy

I love little pussy,
    Her coat is so warm,
And if I don't hurt her
    She'll do me no harm.

So I'll not pull her tail,
    Nor drive her away,
But pussy and I
    Very gently will play.

She shall sit by my side,
    And I'll give her some food;
And pussy will love me
    Because I am good.

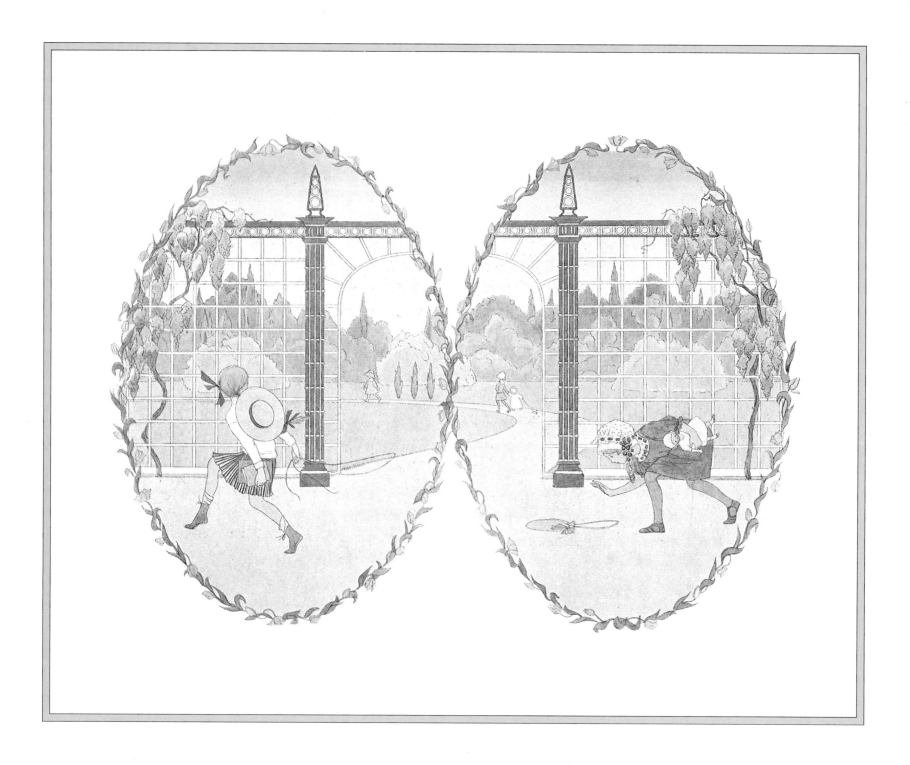

Lucy Locket

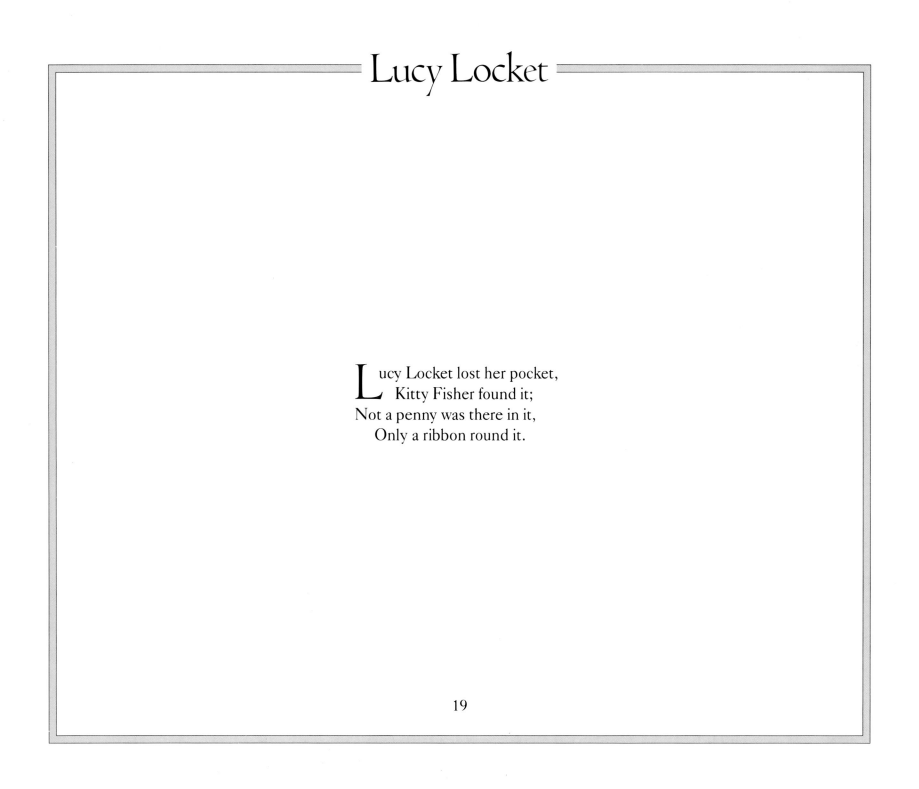

Lucy Locket lost her pocket,
  Kitty Fisher found it;
Not a penny was there in it,
  Only a ribbon round it.

Mary Had a Little Lamb

Mary had a little lamb,
  Its fleece was white as snow;
And everywhere that Mary went
  The lamb was sure to go.

It followed her to school one day,
  That was against the rule;
It made the children laugh and play
  To see a lamb at school.

And so the teacher turned it out,
  But still it lingered near,
And waited patiently about
  Till Mary did appear.

Why does the lamb love Mary so?
  The eager children cry;
Why, Mary loves the lamb, you know,
  The teacher did reply.

Goosey, Goosey, Gander

Goosey, goosey, gander,
Whither shall I wander?
Upstairs and downstairs
And in my lady's chamber.
There I met an old man
Who would not say his prayers.
I took him by the left leg
And threw him down the stairs.

Baa, Baa, Black Sheep

Baa, baa, black sheep,
  Have you any wool?
Yes, sir, yes, sir,
  Three bags full;
One for the master,
  And one for the dame,
And one for the little boy
  Who lives down the lane.

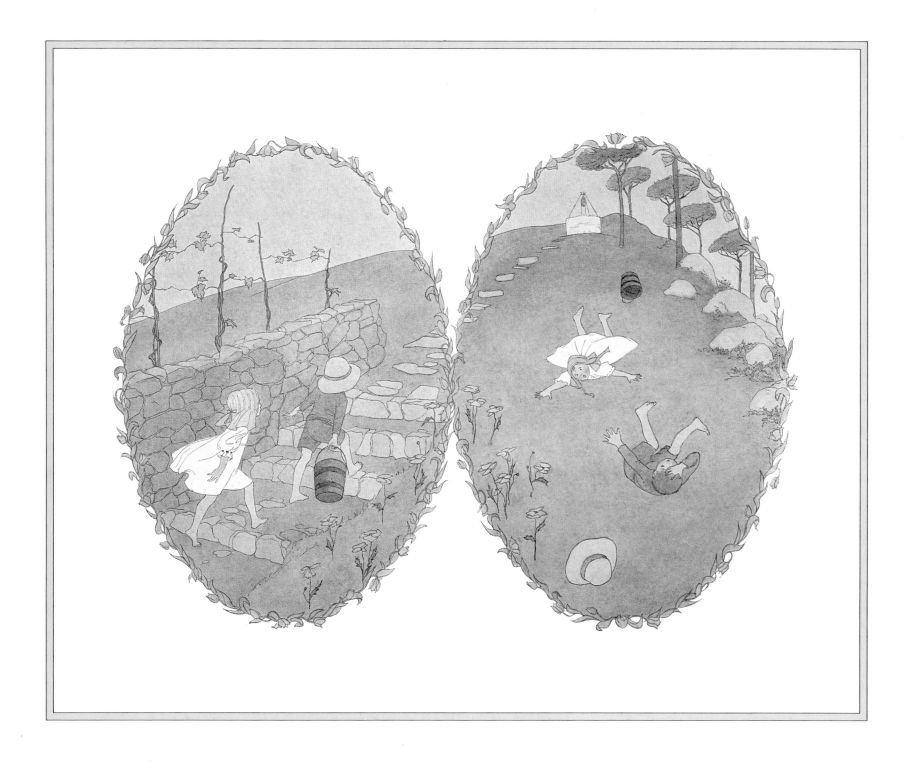

Jack and Jill

Jack and Jill went up the hill
   To fetch a pail of water;
Jack fell down and broke his crown,
   And Jill came tumbling after.
Up Jack got, and home did trot,
   As fast as he could caper,
To old Dame Dob, who patched his nob
   With vinegar and brown paper.

Here We Go Round the Mulberry Bush

Here we go round the mulberry bush,
 The mulberry bush, the mulberry bush,
Here we go round the mulberry bush,
 On a cold and frosty morning.

This is the way we wash our hands,
 Wash our hands, wash our hands,
This is the way we wash our hands,
 On a cold and frosty morning.

This is the way we dry our hands,
 Dry our hands, dry our hands,
This is the way we dry our hands,
 On a cold and frosty morning.

This is the way we clap our hands,
 Clap our hands, clap our hands,
This is the way we clap our hands,
 On a cold and frosty morning.

This is the way we warm our hands,
 Warm our hands, warm our hands,
This is the way we warm our hands,
 On a cold and frosty morning.

The North Wind Doth Blow

The north wind doth blow,
  And we shall have snow,
And what will poor robin do then,
  Poor thing?
He'll sit in a barn,
  And keep himself warm,
And hide his head under his wing,
  Poor thing!

Little Boy Blue

Little Boy Blue,
   Come blow your horn,
The sheep's in the meadow,
   The cow's in the corn.
But where is the boy
   Who looks after the sheep?
He's under a haystack
   Fast asleep.
Will you wake him?
   No, not I,
For if I do, he's sure to cry.

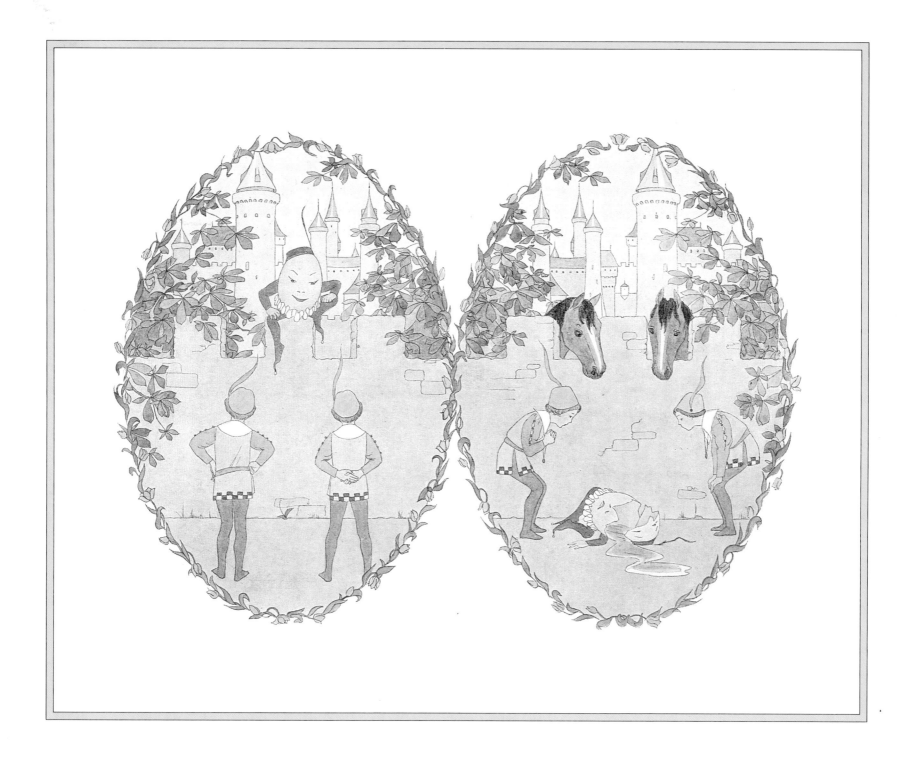

Humpty Dumpty

Humpty Dumpty sat on a wall,
Humpty Dumpty had a great fall.
All the king's horses
And all the king's men,
Couldn't put Humpty together again.

Oh Where, Oh Where Has My Little Dog Gone?

Oh where, oh where has my little dog gone?
Oh where, oh where can he be?
With his ears cut short and his tail cut long,
Oh where, oh where is he?

Dance To Your Daddy

Dance to your daddy,
　My little baby,
Dance to your daddy,
　My little lamb;

You shall have a fishy
　In a little dishy,
You shall have a fishy
　When the boat comes in.

Yankee Doodle

Yankee Doodle came to town,
    Riding on a pony;
He stuck a feather in his cap
    And called it macaroni.
Yankee Doodle, doodle do,
    Yankee Doodle dandy,
All the lasses are so smart,
    And sweet as sugar candy.

Yankee Doodle is a tune
    That comes in mighty handy;
The enemy all runs away
    At Yankee Doodle dandy.
Yankee Doodle, doodle do,
    Yankee Doodle dandy,
All the lasses are so smart,
    And sweet as sugar candy.

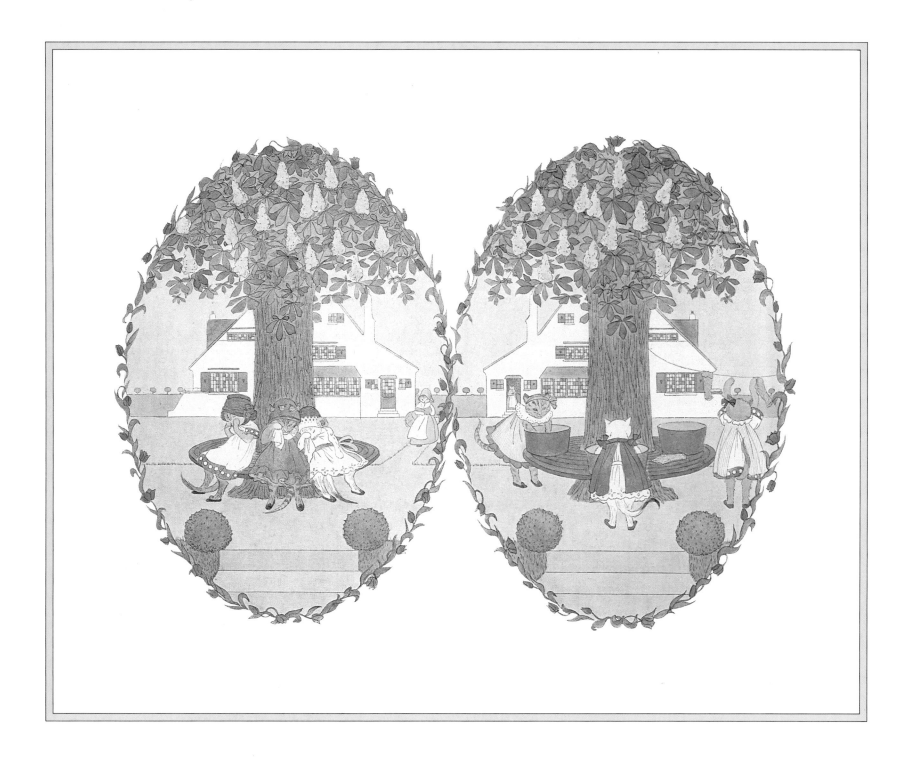

Three Little Kittens

Three little kittens
  They lost their mittens,
And they began to cry,
    Oh, Mother dear, we sadly fear
    Our mittens we have lost.
What! lost your mittens,
You naughty kittens!
    Then you shall have no pie.
    Mee-ow, mee-ow, mee-ow.
No, you shall have no pie.

The three little kittens
They found their mittens,
And they began to cry,
    Oh, Mother dear, see here, see hear,
    Our mittens we have found.
Put on your mittens,
You silly kittens,
    And you shall have some pie.
    Purr-r, purr-r, purr-r,
Oh, let us have some pie.

The three little kittens
Put on their mittens
And soon ate up the pie;
    Oh, Mother dear, we greatly fear
    Our mittens we have soiled.
What! soiled your mittens,
You naughty kittens!
    Then they began to sigh,
    Mee-ow, mee-ow, mee-ow.
Then they began to sigh.

The three little kittens
They washed their mittens,
And hung them out to dry;
    Oh! Mother dear, do you not hear
    Our mittens we have washed.
What! washed your mittens,
Then you're good kittens,
    But I smell a rat close by.
    Mee-ow, mee-ow, mee-ow.
We smell a rat close by.

Three Blind Mice

Three blind mice, see how they run!
They all ran after the farmer's wife,
Who cut off their tails with a carving knife,
Did ever you see such a thing in your life,
As three blind mice?

Young Lambs to Sell

Young lambs to sell!
Young lambs to sell!
I never would cry
Young lambs to sell,
If I'd as much money
As I could tell
I never would cry
Young lambs to sell.

Pussy Cat, Pussy Cat

Pussy cat, pussy cat,
    Where have you been?
I've been to London
    To look at the Queen.
Pussy cat, pussy cat,
    What did you there?
I frightened a little mouse
    Under her chair.

Ding, Dong, Bell

Ding, dong, bell,
   Pussy's in the well.
Who put her in?
   Little Johnny Green.
Who pulled her out?
   Little Tommy Stout.
What a naughty boy was that,
   To try to drown poor pussy cat,
Who never did him any harm
   And killed the mice
In his father's barn.

Georgie Porgie

Georgie Porgie, pudding and pie,
Kissed the girls and made them cry;
When the boys came out to play,
Georgie Porgie ran away.

Ride a Cock Horse

Ride a cock horse
　　To Banbury Cross,
To see a fine lady
　　Upon a white horse;
Rings on her fingers
　　And bells on her toes,
And she shall have music
　　Wherever she goes.

55

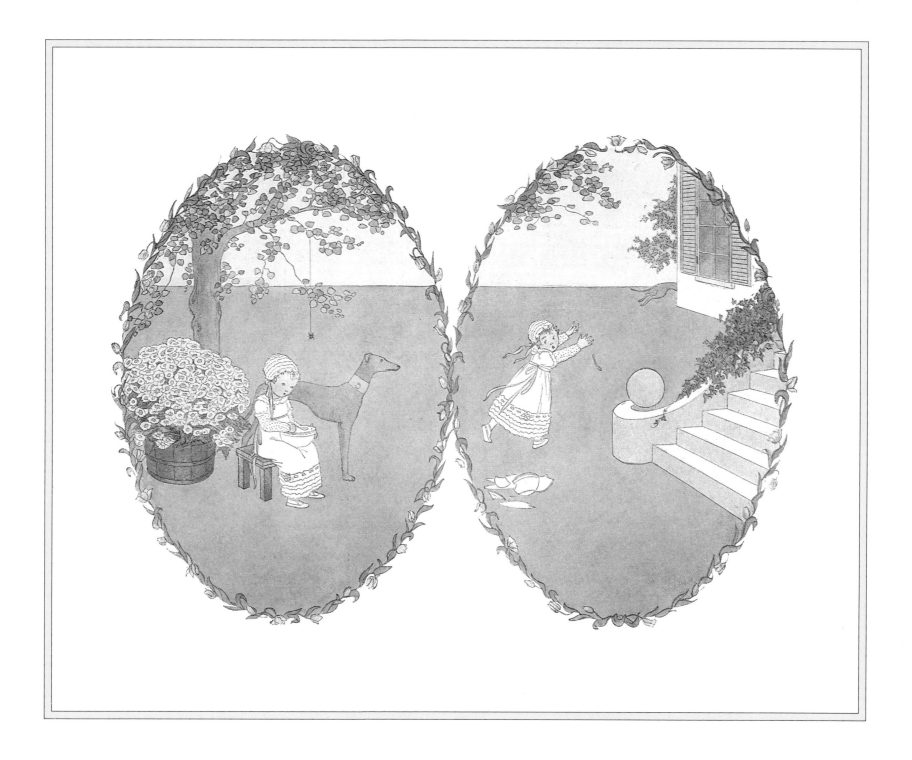

Little Miss Muffett

L ittle Miss Muffet
   Sat on a tuffet,
Eating her curds and whey;
   There came a big spider,
Who sat down beside her
   And frightened Miss Muffet away.

There Was a Little Man

There was a little man,
  And he wooed a little maid,
And he said, Little maid,
  Will you wed, wed, wed?
  I have little more to say,
  Than will you, yea or nay?
For the least said is soonest mended, ded, ded.

Then the little maid replied,
  If I should be your bride,
Pray, what must we have
  For to eat, eat, eat?
  Will the love that you're so rich in
  Make a fire in the kitchen,
And the little god of love turn the spit, spit, spit?

Then the little man he sighed,
  Some say a little cried,
And his little heart was big
  With sorrow, sorrow, sorrow;
  I'll be your little slave,
  And if the little that I have,
Be too little, little dear, I will borrow, borrow, borrow.

Thus did the little gent
  Make the little maid relent,
For her little heart began
  To beat, beat, beat;
  Though his offers were but small,
  She accepted of them all.
Now she thanks her little stars for her fate, fate, fate.

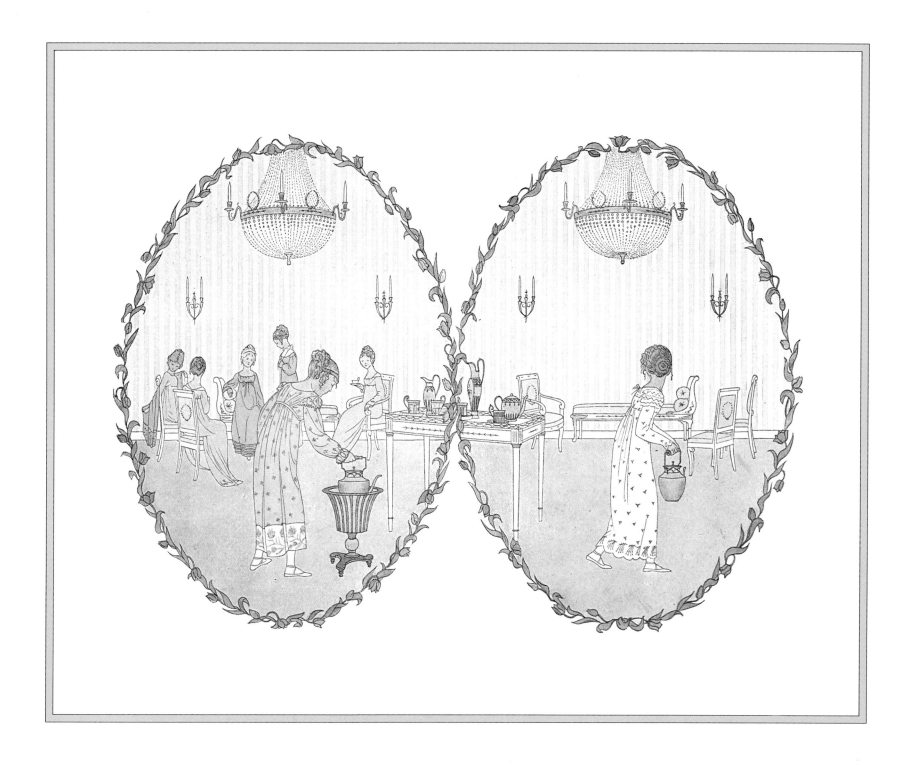

Polly Put the Kettle On

Polly put the kettle on,
   Polly put the kettle on,
Polly put the kettle on,
   We'll all have tea.

Sukey take it off again,
Sukey take it off again,
Sukey take it off again,
   They've all gone away.

Hush-a-Bye Baby

Hush-a-bye, baby,
On the tree top,
When the wind blows
The cradle will rock;
When the bough breaks
The cradle will fall,
Down will come baby,
Cradle and all.

INDEX OF FIRST LINES

B

Baa, baa, black sheep,   25

D

Ding, dong, bell,   51
Dance a baby diddy,   7
Dance to your daddy,   39

G

Goosey, goosey, gander,   23
Georgie Porgie, pudding and pie,   53

H

Hush-a-bye, baby,   63
Here we go round the
    mulberry bush,   29
Humpty Dumpty sat on a wall,   35

I

I love little pussy,   17

J

Jack and Jill went up the hill,   27

L

Little Miss Muffet,   57
Little Boy Blue,   33
Lucy Locket lost her pocket,   19
Little Bo-Peep has lost her
    sheep,   5
Little Jack Horner,   13

M

Mary, Mary, quite contrary,   9
Mary had a little lamb,   21

O

O dear, what can the
    matter be?   15
Oh where, oh where has my
    little dog gone?   37

P

Pussy cat, pussy cat,   49
Polly put the kettle on,   61

R

Ride a cock horse,   55

T

There was a little man,   59
The north wind doth blow,   31
Three little kittens,   43
Three blind mice, see how
    they run!   45

W

What are little boys made of?   11

Y

Young lambs to sell!   47
Yankee Doodle came to town,   41